CRACKERJACK

Youth Literary & Art Magazine

COMPASSION: ISSUE 3
Fall/Winter 2018

Crackerjack Youth & Literary Magazine is published by Kind Eye Publishing, LLC, which is a family owned & operated publishing company that promotes written pieces of work dedicated to the themes of kindness, compassion, inclusion and cross cultural communication. Our dream is to spread understanding through our published material, be it through magazines, essays, manuscripts, self-help books, how-to books and more. Our authors represent a diverse ethnic population and voices that may otherwise be unheard.

Find us online!
www.kindeyepublishing.com
facebook.com/kindeyepublishing

Copyright© 2018 Kind Eye Publishing, LLC All rights reserved
ISBN-13: 978-0999226285 (Kind Eye Publishing, LLC)
ISBN-10: 0999226282

CONTENTS

SHORT STORIES
HENA KACHROO   7
ELISA HEFFERAN   12
KEYA VADIVELU   19

POETRY/LYRICS
BIANCA PATEL   8
ANDREA HEFFERAN   10
PREENA MEHTA   11
NITYA SURI   18

ART
MIKE DEVASSY   9
ZARA GANDHI   11
RALF DEVASSY   13
KAVAN VADIVELU   14
AMRUTHA JULURI   15
DHARMA PATEL   16
GUS HAMMOND   17
REBECA HEFFERAN   COVER, 20

ESSAYS
NAYA PATEL   14
SYAN GANDHI   16

PHOTOGRAPHY
VISHNU JULURI   19

CONTRIBUTORS
ABOUT THE AUTHORS/ARTISTS   21

CRACK·ER·JACK

NOUN: CRACKER-JACK

AN EXCEPTIONALLY GOOD PERSON OR THING : a person or thing of special excellence

COMPASSION

Asking our young contributors, ages 6-18, what "compassion" meant to them was a project that showcased love, happiness, and inclusion. The question elicited joy, bright colors and warm words. Standing up for themselves and each other when they witness pain and destruction. Reaching out a hand to help a new friend, or to stop others behaving badly against old friends. The support and strength given by a dear pet, volunteering to help others in need, rainbows, hearts and inviting hands. These are some of the strong emotions and symbols these crackerjacks came up with when considering compassion.

Just think what these talented kids and the people they reach can do when they show their courage and kindness through ultimate compassion for one another. Being able to exemplify empathy, love and positive action.

They clearly have something to say.

Let's hear these *crackerjacks* out.

Avanti Pradhan Vadivelu
Editor in Chief

Christmas Morning
By Hena Kachroo, 10th grade

It was my 14th Christmas Eve as I sat on the brown leather sofa cuddled up with a soft, checkered blanket. It had aged, with loose strings coming from a few different places, but I liked it all the same. I had the warmth of the fire at my side as I flipped through the pages of my new present. When I finally looked up from my book, I saw the wind in flurries, blowing sugar white snow off the ground and into the air. I remember, when I was 5 years old, Marlene came home for Christmas and we spent the whole day together, outside, in the snow just having fun. The fact that our toes were about to fall off didn't stop us. That day, was one of the best days of my life. But that was then and this is now, and my sister hasn't come to visit like that since then. Right before she was about to leave, she got into a fight with our parents about them wanting her to visit more often. I stood there watching them yell at each other, hoping I wouldn't lose the only sister I had. But I had already lost her. She turned, stormed out the front door, and never looked back. From that night on my parents took it on themselves to work more often. They left before I woke, and came back after I slept. I knew I lost a sister that night, but I didn't realize I had lost my parents too.

It was about 10:40pm when I figured I had had enough of The Great Gatsby. I usually only had the company of my books. Every Christmas my parents would get me a new book as if to make up for all the time lost to work. But it never could. This year they got me The Great Gatsby. Like every other year, my parents were late coming home, so I unwrapped my book knowing that tomorrow would be another forgotten Christmas.

As I walked up the stairs, the wooden floorboards creaked beneath my feet. I got to my bed in the second room on the left, and I just laid there. I laid there for what seemed like a couple minutes, but when my mom walked through the door I knew it had been a couple hours. "Mary?" she yelled from downstairs. But I didn't answer, I never did and she knew that. By the time my dad came back I was still awake. In fact, I didn't seem to get any sleep that night. All I could think about was how another Christmas would be gone and nothing would have changed.

I knew it was early morning when I heard the car engine running. My parents were about to leave for work. When I heard the sound of my door open, I saw my mom's shadow. She was peeking through the slit in my door to see if I was asleep, so I closed my eyes and pretended that nothing was wrong, for her sake and for mine. But it was Christmas morning and I had no one to share it with. I went downstairs like it was a regular day. Since I had already opened my present last night, I didn't spare a glance at the Christmas tree.

That day, I did everything as I normally would. Except for one thing. I decided to take a walk because … well I don't know. But after I finished the little coffee my parents left over, I went outside. As I walked, I left deep imprints in the snow. I took long breaths while I admired all the rooftops covered in blankets of the white powder. There was even a little breeze, but I didn't shy away. I liked the touch of the cold air against my pale skin. I continued on for many long minutes until I realized someone was following me. I turned to see a little girl.

She seemed to be about 7, had curly dark brown hair, and big eyes the color of dark chocolate. She gave me a puzzled look as if to ask why I stopped walking. I asked her what her name was and where her parents were but she just kept staring at me.

(Continues on next page)

After a couple minutes she said, "My name is Alisa, and my parents are working", as if she had decided she could trust me. I wondered why her parents would leave her alone if she was only 7 but I decided not to ask about that, yet. I continued walking and she told me more about herself. She told me that her parents have to work a lot and that they often leave her alone but she could take care of herself. I doubted that last part but urged her to continued. She also told me that her parents had left early this morning and had not left her anything under the tree. I immediately turned around to catch her surprised at my motion. I realized the whole time we had been walking, she had been following in my footsteps, placing her foot exactly where I had placed mine. "Your parents left? And they didn't leave anything for you?" I said, with a little sadness in my voice. No one deserved to be alone on Christmas. But she just shrugged like it was no big deal. As if she was used to it. "Well we better change that then shouldn't we?" she looked up from her feet so fast I almost jumped. We walked back to my house to grab the little money I had saved up from little jobs I had done around the neighborhood. It wasn't much, but if it was enough to get Alisa what she wanted for Christmas, it was worth spending. We walked to the store and she picked out The Giver which, I was surprised by. Normal 7-year-old girls would pick out dolls or stuffed animals, but I guess she liked reading. I paied for it and then spent the rest of the day with Alisa, reading. It wasn't a big gesture, but she reminded me of myself, and if I could help her feel better, then maybe I could help my family too.

Ways to be Compassionate
By Bianca Patel, 3rd grade

Compassion is helping a friend
A friend that is hurt
Compassion is helping others
Helping someone carry something
Compassion is caring
Giving attention when someone is sad
Compassion is sharing
Sharing toys with a new friend
Compassion is being friendly
Offering a seat on the bus to someone new
Compassion is playing with someone
Inviting someone lonely to play

I think that the first act of compassion is that a mother gives birth to you. She does not just reject you.
By Mike Devassy, 5th grade

Bystander
By Andrea Hefferan, 11th grade

They call her
Ugly
Fat
Stupid

Me,
I don't see it.
To me, she's brilliant

But I never tell her
I want to so badly
I just don't want to be
Ugly
Fat
Stupid

Every time they see her
They point
They whisper
Some don't even
Lower their voices at all

Ugly
Ugly
Ugly
Ugly
Ugly

Fat
Fat
Fat
Fat
Fat

Stupid
Stupid
Stupid
Stupid
Stupid

UglyFatStupidUglyFatStupidUglyFatStupid

Every day

Luckily
She is strong
She never seems to listen
That makes them yell louder

One day
I see it
In the corner of her eye

A single tear.

They do get to her after all
But I sit there watching
As it slides down her face
Onto her hand
It is about to hit the floor

I've had it.
I stand up abruptly
Knocking over my chair in my haste
Running up to her
I face her tormentors
And I tell them

stop

They laugh
I shrink

Then
A clatter
Someone stands up

And joins us

Someone else
And someone else
More and more people join until
They are outnumbered
And we tell them

STOP.

I was a Girl Scout last year, and I went to Matthew 25 Ministries, a humanitarian aid organization, with my troop. I saw all the floods, hurricanes, earthquakes, and tornadoes that were happening. I also saw the tiny homes that the people in those regions lived in, and it made me very sad. Our troop donated gloves to the volunteers so they could fix the homes without getting splinters. That made me feel like I was making a difference in someone's life, it also made me feel lucky for everything that I have in my life and appreciate it.

By Zara Gandhi, 3rd grade

Compassion
By Preena Mehta

Compassion is thinking and concerning about other people.

Compassion is helping others through misfortune.

Compassion is helping others in need.

Being compassionate means everything to others in need!

Birds of Compassion
By Elisa Hefferan, 4th grade

I don't know what made me talk to the new girl at my school. Maybe it was because she looked so odd, lonely, and out of place in this dull, grey boring school with her red hair and red dress. Maybe it was because Caroline Wang, the class gossip, was spreading rumors about the new girl. Or maybe it was because I felt lost in this big school, the school I knew so well, because Cecilia, my best friend, moved to a new school, Brookhood. So while Mrs. Kanis took attendance, I studied the new girl, who did nothing interesting besides look at her shoes and bite her lip a dozen times. However, I was so interested in the NG, (Abbreviation for new girl,) Mrs. Kanis had to say my name four times before I finally realized she'd been screaming in my face. "Wait, what huh?" I said in one breath. "Miss. Randrea Martin, you're clearly not paying any attention in the slightest!" Mrs. Kanis's face loomed unpleasantly close to mine, making me endure the smell of her horrid perfume. I winced, and twirled my blue hair around, avoiding eye contact. "Uh… here?" I squeaked. "Better." Mrs. K, giving me one last final glare, turned around with a swish of her glossy brown hair. I sighed with relief, though soon it turned to a sigh of annoyance. "Hello, Miss Big nose." Caroline Wang was once again, sticking her abnormally long nose into others business. "Oh, Miss French has a grumpy attitude today!" She smirked. Oh, wait! Did I forget to mention I'm French? Well, I speak English perfectly, I just have a French accent. Some people tease me about it, and when I say some, I mean Caroline and her gang of giggly girls. Caroline was now beginning to rant about something, so I tuned out of the conversation. I glanced at the NG. I expected her to be staring at me, but to my surprise, she had her head down on her desk, as though she had done something wrong. Poor girl! She probably felt so scared, small and lonely… I blinked twice in surprise, for a sudden thought occurred me. Was that how Cecilia felt? Scared, lost, and lonely… I drifted off for the rest of homeroom, thinking of Cecilia, NG, and how was Mrs. K going to punish me this time, for not paying attention. Again.

    Before I knew it, homeroom was over, and Mrs. K was screaming to me about daydreaming or something like that. Huh. I don't remember ever daydreaming. Oh wait, when I was thinking about Cecilia and the NG? That's when I daydreamed? No, you got it wrong. I don't daydream, I merely think. While not paying attention to whatever someone's saying. Very different. Just to stay on the safe side though, I hurried quickly to my next class, math. On my way there, I saw the NG, walking like she was in slow motion. I quickly caught up to her. Her face was pale with fear, or maybe it was just always pale. She looked timid and nervous, and wasn't even trying at all to put a smile on her face. "Poor thing" I murmured. I placed a steady hand on her arm. "It's kind of hard to be lonely in such a big school, don't you think so?" The new girl stopped right in her tracks and turned to face me. Her bright green eyes were as wide as saucers. "Um… yeah…well… ah…hi…" She stammered. I smiled at her, showing her my turquoise braces. "Hi. My name is Randrea, what's yours?" For a moment she just stayed silent, not saying a word. Then she replied softly, tugging on a loose strand of hair. "Ana…Anabeca" "Nice name!" "Yeah…thanks…where are your other friends?" This time it was my time to tug a loose strand of hair. "Oh, my friend moved, to a school called Brookhood, I think." I paused "She was a good friend, Cecilia was her name." I paused again. "Well, what good is it just standing here? Let's go! What's your next class?" "Math" Anabeca answered, now smiling. "Cool! Same here!" I grinned, knowing this day was going to be great. I don't know if Anabeca noticed, but I felt my eyes widen in surprise and I emitted a gasp, for behind me I heard a peal of merry laughter.

(Continues on next page)

"This day keeps getting better and better!' I thought. The school day seemed to go so quickly, and now Anabeca and I were on the bus. We were in the same neighborhood, did I mention that? "You know, your hair and your dress kind of remind of a bright red cardinal." I observed. Anabeca blushed and looked up at her red wavy hair, then at her bright red dress. Talk about loving red! "I have a great idea!" I announced. "What is it?" Anabeca asked nervously, twisting her hands in her lap.

"Since you remind me of a cardinal, your nickname should be Cardinal!" I told Anabeca excitedly. "Yeah! And your nickname should be..." she stopped and looked up at my funky, blue, ponytail. "Your nickname should be Blue Jay!" Anabeca, I mean, Cardinal. nearly shouted. "Okay, Cardinal. Blue Jay sounds cool." I responded, winking. "Nice choice, Blue Jay" She replied, winking back. We both bursted out of laughter. We were both giggling delightfully when I stopped giggling. "Can you be my new best friend?" I asked, hoping this wasn't too sudden. "What?" Cardinal asked, and she too stopped giggling. "I would love to, but isn't Cecilia already your best friend?" she asked. I smiled. "Well, yeah, but I can have more than one best friend, right?" I said eagerly. Cardinal nodded. "Well, what do you say?" I asked. I sounded brave, but I felt jittery. Cardinal smiled

"YES!" She said loudly. And she jumped up and hugged me. We started cracking up again. A boy who was sitting behind us peeked over the seat, scowling. "Be quiet!" He barked. Cardinal stopped laughing, startled. I made a funny face at her. She couldn't resist a grin. Then a giggle. Then she started laughing, hard. The guy behind us cried "Stop, stop, stop!" But we couldn't stop. Oh, yes, this was definitely a very good day.

I saw a mother elephant standing near her baby when he was sleeping.

By Ralf Devassy, 2nd grade

By Kavan Vadivelu, 6th grade

A Full Bucket
By Naya Patel, 2nd grade

Someone got hurt at school. She was my friend and I helped her up and asked if she needed to go to the nurse. I went to the nurse because she was bleeding and I care about people. I am compassionate because I do not like people to get hurt. I care because I want to fill their "bucket". If their "bucket" is filled all the way up then that means they will be very happy.

This bucket concept is sourced from *The Invisible Bucket*.

"Compassion means to light up someone's heart when they get hurt."

By Amrutha Juluri, 4th grade

Showing Compassion
By Syan Gandhi, 5th grade

If someone shows compassion they are showing kindness or caring. Compassion is a deep awareness of and sympathy for another's feelings, and a humane quality of understanding the suffering of others and wanting to do something about it.

If there was no compassion, people would be mean to each other. They wouldn't help each other, and they wouldn't care about one another.

One can show compassion by helping others such as giving food to the poor, caring for plants and animals, helping your parents, caring for the sick, or just being there for a friend in need.

I've showed compassion by helping my friends by teaching them something new to help them on a test. I've also showed compassion by helping the poor by packaging toiletries, food, and giving food and toys to an animal shelter. It is rewarding to feel that I made a difference, and that makes me want to continue being that way.

By Dharma Patel, 10th grade

I chose to paint a portrait of my dog Kevin to represent compassion. I chose Kevin to represent compassion because as a dog, he is kind, loving, and caring. He makes me feel loved, happy, and cared for.

By Gus Hammond, 6th grade

Compassionate Heart
Lyrics By Nitya Suri, 8th grade

(Verse)
Once upon a time
A long time ago
A girl with long hair
A guy with a horse
She lived in a tower
Waiting to see th stars
He lived with the pandits only gold in his thoughts
When fate came along
The two collided
She asked him to take her to the stars

(Pre-Chorus)
Everyone has
A different love story
A different one
In their heart
But you will find
In every love story
A kind, pure heart

(Chorus)
So keep gold in your heart
Your heart, your heart
Keet it out of your head
Your head, your head
Make sure to start
To start to start
With a compassionate heart
Live with your heart
Your heart, your heart
But also use your head
Your head, your head
Make sure to use
Your compassionate heart

(Verse)
The next story here
In one I'm sure you know
A prince in his palace
A girl a slave at home
He wishes for a wife
Who he can love til the end
She wishes for the ball, the ball
So she can go and dance
Well she goes, then she runs
A loses a shoe
So he finds her using that clue

(Pre-Chorus)
Everyone has
A different love story
A different one
In their heart
But you will find
In every love story
A kind, pure heart

(Chorus)
So keep gold in your heart
Your heart, your heart
Keet it out of your head
Your head, your head
Make sure to start
To start to start
With a compassionate heart
Live with your heart
Your heart, your heart
But also use your head
Your head, your head
Make sure to use
Your compassionate heart

(Verse)
You see, you know the stories well
Been told them since you're young
You looked up to their stories
How brave all of them had been
Dressed up as them for Halloween
You wanted to be them
It's easier than you think

(Chorus)
Just keep gold in your heart
Your heart, your heart
Keep it out of your head
Your head, your head
Make sure to start
To start to start
With a compassionate heart
Live with your heart
Your heart, your heart
But also use your head
Your head, your head
Make sure to use

To use
That compassionate heart
Your compassionate HEART

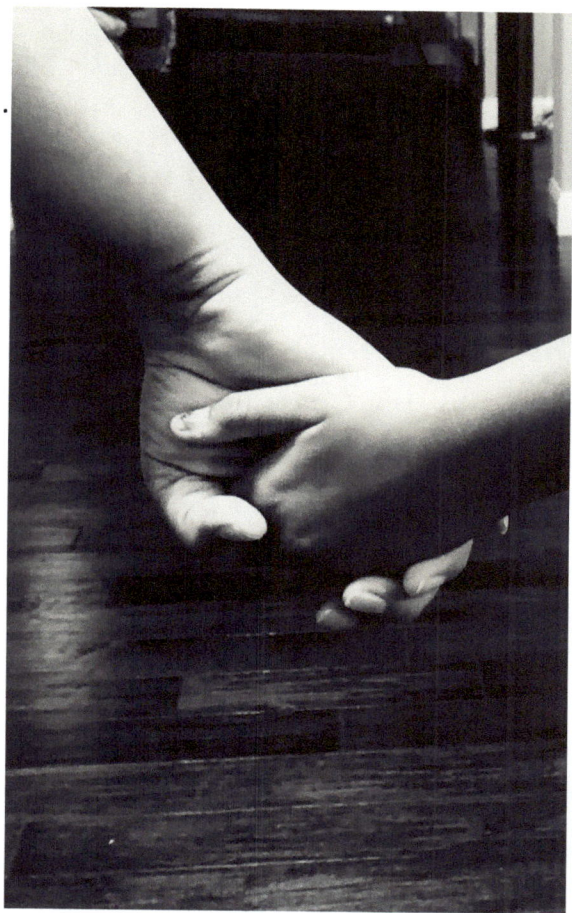

"Compassion is offering a helping hand"
By Vishnu Juluri, 3rd grade

Mavey and Her Problems: Being Nice to the Mean
By Keya Vadivelu, 4th grade

    Mavey was proud of herself, because she stood up for herself, and yet didn't realize that she used hurtful words. "Mavey, I need to talk to you about how you reacted to Addison and Ellie," said Mavey's mom. "Okay mom, is there a camera or something set up down there, because I did pretty great reacting to Addison and Ellie," yelled Mavey from upstairs. Mavey raced her brother down the stairs. "What is going on, Mavey?" said Mavey's little brother, Ben. "Go next door Ben, Babysitter Lacy will drop you off at school," said Mavey's mom to Ben. "Before I leave I just want to tell you to not use hurtful words to people even when you are going against bullies. Because if you do, you yourself will sound like a bully, and you aren't one so don't act like that. At school I want you to say sorry to them about the hurtful words. Bye Honey, have fun at school!"

    When Mavey was at school she told Addison and Ellie sorry, Mavey a tear sprinkled down her face. She went to the nurse because she wouldn't talk. The nurse talked to her to see if anything was bothering her, Mavey did not speak so she went back to class and she wrote her thoughts down and gave it to the teacher. After that day she went back to normal and never used hurtful words again.

"Here For You"

By Rebeca Hefferan, 9th grade

CRACKERJACK CONTRIBUTORS

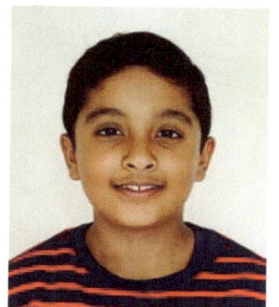

Mike Devassy, Artist

I just love to read. My current interest is Mythology (esp. Greek). In my spare time, I like to bike and play badminton. Our passion as a family is traveling. I recently traveled to the birth place of Legos- Billund, Denmark. I also love playing the guitar. They say I play well. If I am not reading then I am playing Soccer or building with Legos.

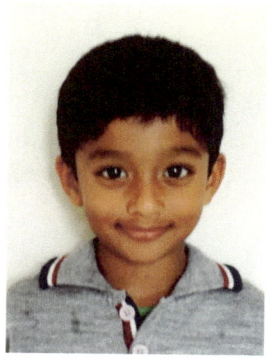

Ralf Devassy, Artist

I am an eight year old. I love cars. I collect Hot wheels cars. I enjoy building with Legos. Soccer is my favorite game. I played it since I was three years old. I love reading about animals. Someday I want to travel around the world and study animals.

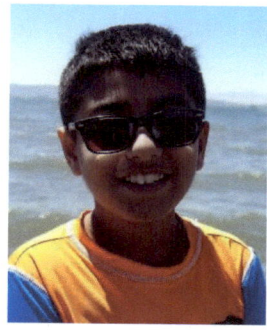

Syan Gandhi, Columnist

I am a witty 5th grader, who loves to read. I am a nature lover, and enjoy spending time outdoors hiking, creeking, and collecting bugs/rocks.

Zara Gandhi, Artist

I am a sassy 3rd grader, who loves art. I am passionate about gymnastics, hiking, and appreciating nature.

Gus Hammond, Artist

My name is Gus and I am in the 6th grade. I love to play water polo and paint. I am also in boy scouts and I really love to camp and be outside. I love my dog, Kevin, and I like to take him on walks and play with him.

Andrea Hefferan, Poet

I am a junior at Mason High School. I enjoy reading and writing very much. I write for her high school's newspaper, The Chronicle. Playing music is one of my favorite activities; I play the violin and piano. In my free time, you can find my reading a book or listening to songs from the musical Hamilton.

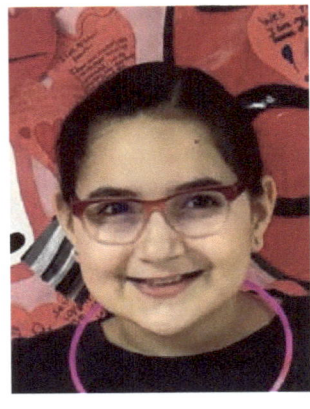

Elisa Hefferan, Short Story Writer

I am a fourth grader at Mason City Schools and love writing, reading, and drawing. I also enjoy roller skating, dancing, and playing the piano. I have two sisters and an amazing mom and dad. I have some wonderful friends who always support me. This is my second publication for Crackerjack.

Rebeca Hefferan, Artist

I am a ninth grader at Mason City Schools and am a middle child with an older and younger sister. I enjoy reading, writing and drawing in my free time. I love history and science, and I love listening to music. I am always doodling on something, and never far away from a creative idea.

Hena Kachroo, Short Story Writer

My name is Hena Kachroo and I am a sophomore at Lafayette High School. I write for the Lafayette Times newspaper as well as the newsletter for the Bluegrass Indo-American Civic Society. Along with writing, I do Indian classical dance called Barathnatyam, which I have been doing for around ten years now.

Amrutha Juluri, Artist

I am a 9 year old artist. Music, art and time with friends and family are the keys to my happiness.

Vishnu Juluri, Photo Editor

I am an avid sports fan and player of many sports. I also enjoy playing with dogs, the theater and Bollywood dance.

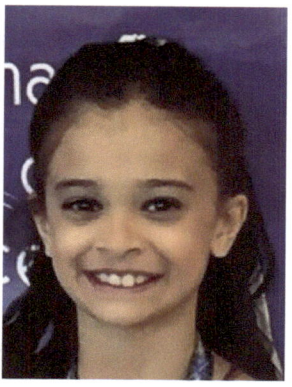

Preena Mehta, Poet

I am a fifth grader at Mason City Schools and enjoys playing sports, doing crafts, and hanging out with her friends. She lives at home with her mom, dad, brother and "little sister" puppy.

Bianca Patel, Poet

I was born in Louisville Kentucky on April 24, 2010 and moved when I was a baby to Mason, Ohio. My family members include my mom, dad, little sister and little brother. Almost my entire family lives in Georgia, of which I am the oldest cousin. I love to read, dance, play tennis and play with my friends.

Dharma Patel, Artist

I am a sophomore at William Mason High School in Ohio. I am a competitive jump roper for the Comet Skippers and am involved in a couple of clubs at school. I love to travel and have been on many mission/volunteer trips, which I enjoy so much!

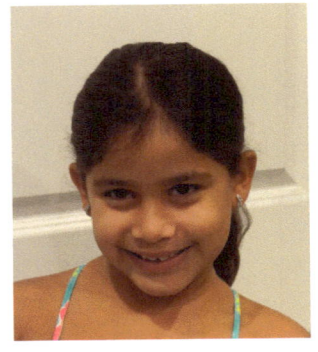

Naya Patel, Columnist

I am six years old and I am in 2nd grade. I like to play with my friends, do back bends and dance. I love to eat pizza and candy.

Nitya Suri, Lyricist

I am the one and only Nitya Suri. Being 13 and in 8th grade, I've heard the word "compassion" a lot. I believe that it's doing it with your heart. I've been singing and dancing for as long as I can remember and I love it because I do it with my everything. So that's why writing a song about compassion just felt right. I have so much fun writing up songs and thinking up tunes, and I hope someday I might share it with the world. Without music it's just words on a page, I can't put sounds on paper, but I wish to perform it one day!

Kavan Vadivelu, Artist

I am a 6th grader and love soccer and theater. This coming winter I will be appearing as "Mowgli" in the Children's Theatre of Cincinnati's professional production of The Jungle Book at the Taft Theater. I love to draw and consider it a way to relax.

Keya Vadivelu, Short Story Writer

I am a 4th grader and enjoy putting together outfits, singing, journaling and making up plays. I'm always coming up with something new and most recently have taken up jump roping competitively and playing the cello.

Thanks to all our Crackerjack Contributors! We look forward to our next issue, "FREEDOM" !

Follow us on social media for updates, or sign up to be on our mailing list for the latest information.

Check out these Kind Eye Publishing titles now available for purchase! Use the code **"CRACKERJACK"** for a special discount for all Crackerjack fans!

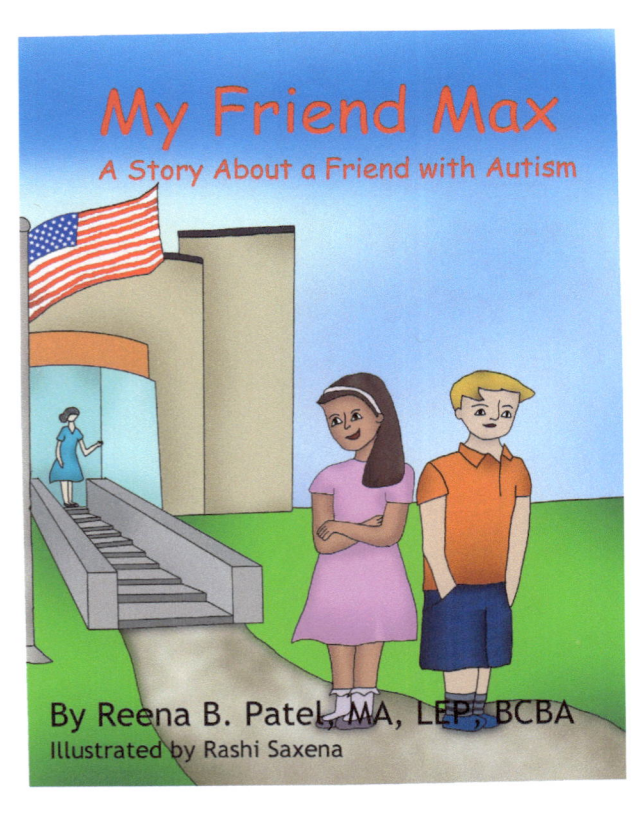

www.ingramcontent.com/pod-product-compliance
Lightning Source LLC
Chambersburg PA
CBHW040023050426
42452CB00002B/114